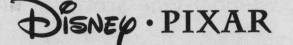

Disney · PIXAR

ULTIMATE MOVIE MIX

Featuring your favorite Disney · PIXAR characters!

A GOLDEN BOOK • NEW YORK

Copyright © 2006 Disney Enterprises, Inc./Pixar. Disney/Pixar elements © Disney/Pixar; Hudson Hornet is a trademark of DaimlerChrysler; Volkswagen trademarks, design patents and copyrights are used with the approval of the owner, Volkswagen AG; Model T is a registered trademark of Ford Motor Company; Fiat is a trademark of Fiat S.p.A.; Mack is a registered trademark of Mack Trucks, Inc.; Chevrolet Impala is a trademark of General Motors; Porsche is a trademark of Porsche; Jeep is a registered trademark of DaimlerChrysler; Plymouth Superbird is a trademark of DaimlerChrysler. Sarge's rank insignia design used with the approval of the U.S. Army. Petty marks used by permission of Petty Marketing LLC. All rights reserved. Published in the United States by Golden Books, an imprint of Random House Children's Books, a division of Random House, Inc., New York, in conjunction with Disney Enterprises, Inc. Golden Books, A Golden Book, and the G colophon are registered trademarks of Random House, Inc. Originally published in slightly different form as four different works under the titles *Kid-tastrophe!*, written by Rebecca Gomez, illustrated by Denise Shimabukuro, Lori Tyminksi, and the Disney Storybook Artists, copyright © 2001 Disney Enterprises, Inc./Pixar Animation Studios, published by Random House, Inc., in 2001; *Swim Team*, adapted by Jasmine Jones, illustrated by the Disney Storybook Artists, copyright © 2003 Disney Enterprises, Inc./Pixar Animation Studios, published by Random House, Inc., in 2003; *Supers [to the] Rescue!*, adapted by Cary Okmin, illustrated by the Disney Storybook Artists, copyright © 2004 Disney Enterprises, Inc./Pixar Animation Studios, published by Random House, Inc., in 2004; *Welcome to Radiator Springs*, [by] Cynthia Hands, illustrated by the Disney Storybook Artists, copyright © 2006 Disney Enterprises, Inc./P[ixar].

www.goldenbooks.com
www.randomhouse.com/kids/disney
ISBN-13: 978-0-7364-2415-8
ISBN-10: 0-7364-2415-6
Printed in the United States of America
10 9 8 7 6 5 4

Sulley is the Number One Scarer at Monsters, I

Mike is his assistant. Scarers collect screams that are turned into power for the city of Monstropolis.

Mike's girlfriend is Celia. She has snakes on her head instead of hair. Circle the picture that is different.

A.

B.

C.

D.

E.

Randall is a Scarer, too. He can disappear by blending into things. How many R's can you find hidden in the picture?

Answer: 5.

Roz is in charge of paperwork. Mike never
does his, and that makes Roz mad.

The top Scarers walk onto the Scare Floor.

The closet doors on the Scare Floor lead into kids' rooms.

Monsters are scared of kids. They think kids' belongings will hurt them! To find out what's scaring these monsters, unscramble the letters and write them in the spaces below.

A   C   K   S   O

_ _ _ _ _

Sulley and Mike put kids' screams in special cans. How many words can you make using the letters found in SCREAM?
(Use each letter only once in each word.)

_____ _____

_____ _____

_____ _____

_____

_____

_____

Possible answers: Am, are, came, care, cream, ear, me, race, ram, sea.

The Child Detection Agency (CDA) keeps monsters safe from kids' stuff. They arrive to take away the dangerous sock!

Waternoose is the head of Monsters, Inc. He asks Sulley to show the new Scarers how to be scary.

Roz is upset because Mike didn't finish his paperwork. Sulley tells Mike he'll finish it for him.

When Sulley goes back up to Mike's desk, he sees
a door. Then he hears something behind him.
To find out what it is, circle every third letter. Then
write the letters in order on the spaces below.

C X A N Q K B R I Z M D

___ ___ ___ ___ ___

Answer: A KID.

Oh, no! A kid is in the monster world!

Monstropolis is in danger! Sulley has to put the kid back in her own world.

**Mike and Celia are out to dinner
when Sulley appears in the window.**

Sulley wants to show Mike the kid . . .

. . . but she has already gotten away!
All the monsters scream and run outside.

Mike and Sulley are scared of the kid.

When the girl screams, the lights go on and off. When she laughs, the lights glow even brighter. Mike's apartment is mixed up, and that makes the kid giggle. Can you find everything that is wrong?

Answers: Mike's lamp is an umbrella; there is a plate on the chair; the clock on the wall has legs and feet; the vase on the table has lollipops in it.

The kid draws a picture of a monster she's afraid of. It's Randall!

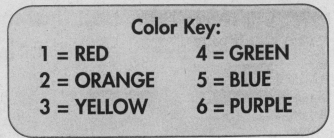

Color Key:

1 = RED   4 = GREEN

2 = ORANGE   5 = BLUE

3 = YELLOW   6 = PURPLE

Sulley doesn't think the girl will hurt them.
Mike doesn't agree with him.

The next day, Sulley and Mike take the girl to
Monsters, Inc., so they can put her back in her room.

Sulley and Mike are looking for the girl's door to send her home, but they have the wrong one! Find her door. (Hint: It's the one that is different.)

Sulley calls the girl Boo. Mike is angry. He can't believe Sulley has given the girl a name!

Boo has disappeared. Sulley runs to look for her.

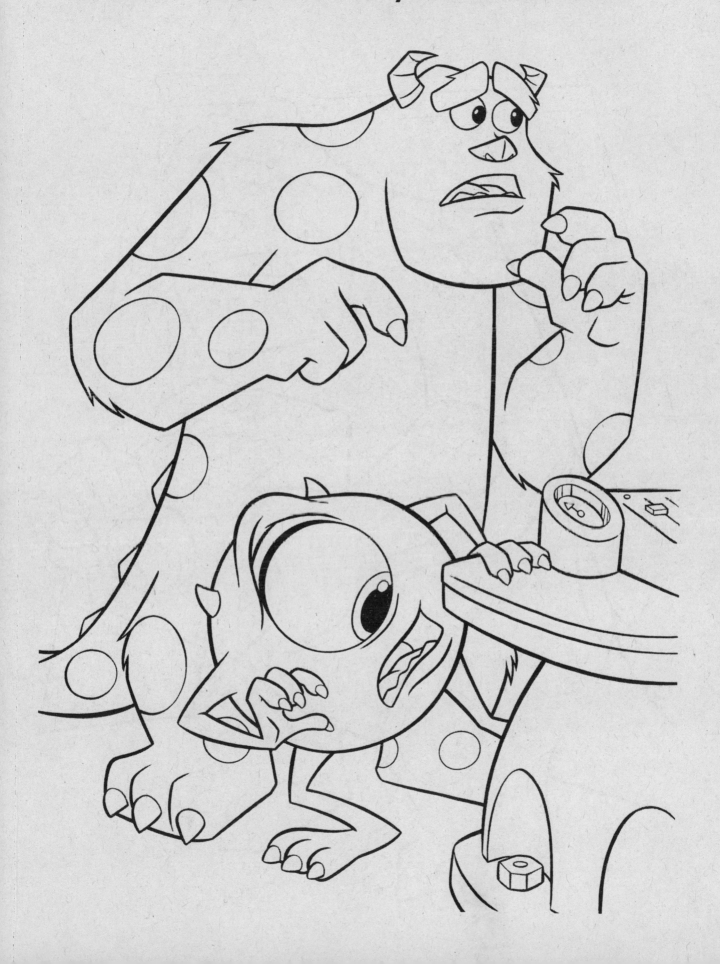

Sulley thinks Boo is gone forever.

Sulley hears Boo's voice! Which monster is she?

Sulley is glad that Boo is safe.

Mike catches up with Sulley and Boo and tells them to follow him. To find out where he takes them, tilt the top of the page downward, close one eye, and view the message from the bottom of the page.

Randall has put Boo's door back. Sulley doesn't trust Randall, so Mike walks right into Boo's room to prove that everything is safe.

Randall sets a trap for Boo . . .

. . . but he catches Mike by mistake!

Boo finds a secret door that leads to Randall's hideout!

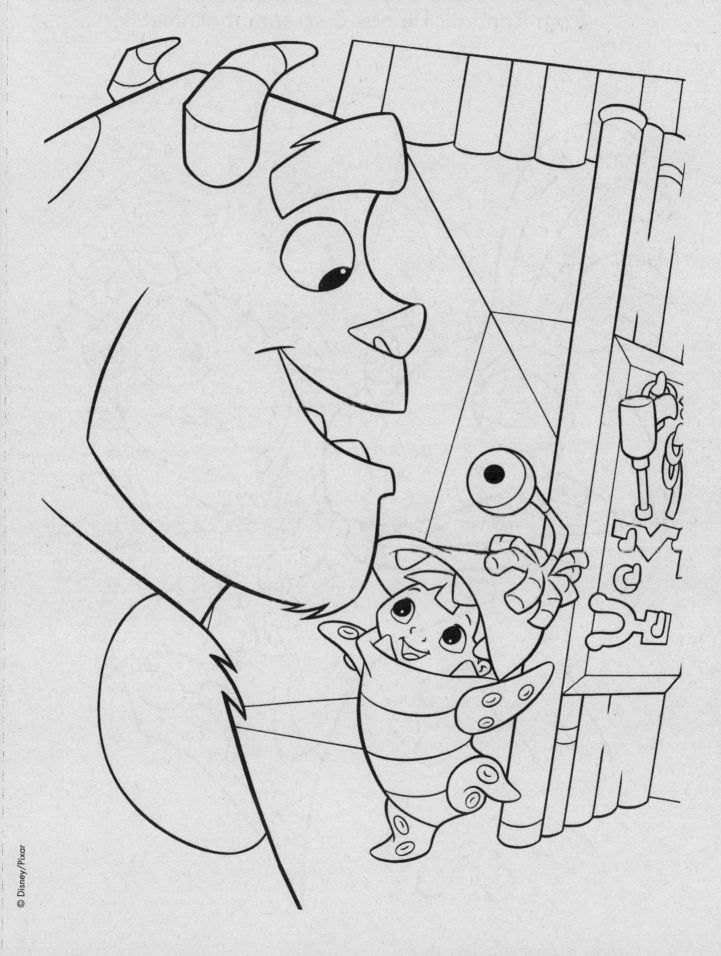

Sulley and Boo find Mike. They all run away
from Randall. He has a scream machine!

Sulley wants to tell Waternoose what has
happened. The boss won't listen. Waternoose asks
Sulley to teach the new Scarers how to roar.

Sulley's roar scares Boo.

Waternoose is mad because Sulley and Mike have brought a kid into the monster world. He and Randall grab Boo . . .

. . . and Waternoose sends Sulley
and Mike into the human world.

Mike thinks they'll never get home.

Mike is mad at Sulley. He throws a snowball at him.

**Mike and Sulley make a new friend,
who tells them that there is a town nearby.**

Sulley has an idea. Connect the dots to find out what he builds.

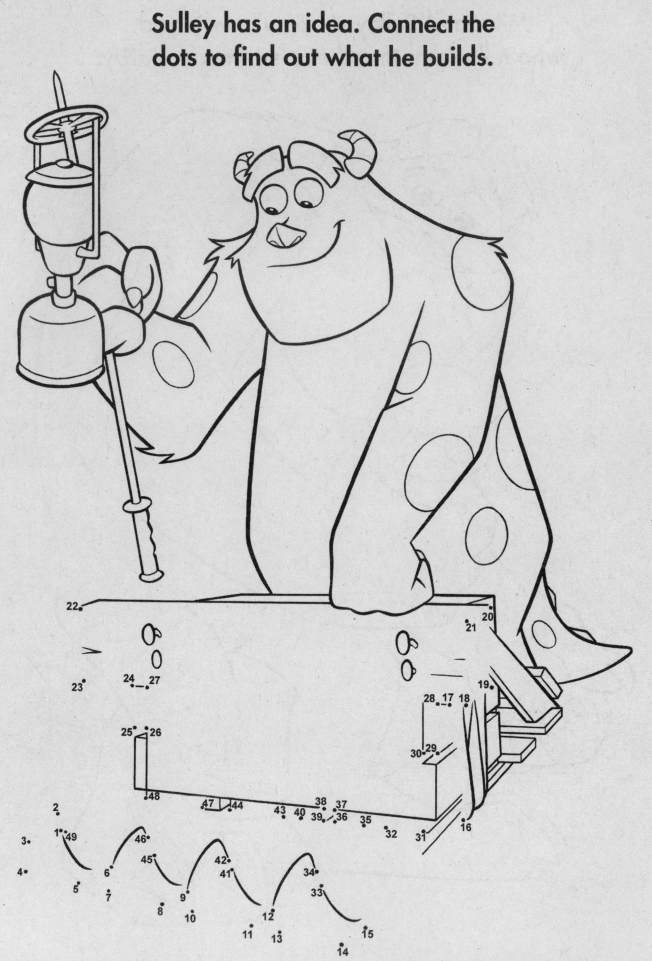

Sulley knows that if he can get to a town, he can go back to the monster world through a kid's closet door. Help him find the path that leads to the town.

START

STOP!

FINISH

Sulley finds a town—and a kid's door!

Sulley rescues Boo from Waternoose and Randall!

Mike catches up with Sulley. He can't tell that Randall has made himself invisible and is hitting his friend!

Mike, Sulley, and Boo run away from Randall.
But Randall won't give up! He doesn't want them
to tell anyone about his scream machine.

Celia helps Mike by playing a trick on Randall.
How many C's can you find?

Sulley wants Mike to run! Can you find everything that begins with the letter M?

Answer: Mike, milk, mitt, monsters, mop, muffin.

Mike and Sulley want to get Boo back to her door.
But Randall chases them through lots of doors.

How many doors can you count?

Answer: 10.

Boo laughs. Her laugh is more powerful than
a scream. Now they can open the doors!

Boo isn't afraid of Randall anymore.
Sulley and Mike send him into the human world.

Uh-oh! Waternoose brings Boo's door back to the Scare Floor.

Waternoose has chased Sulley and Boo into a room. Waternoose tells Sulley his plan to get more screams. To find out his plan, begin at the center and write down the letters in the spaces below in the order they appear around the spiral.

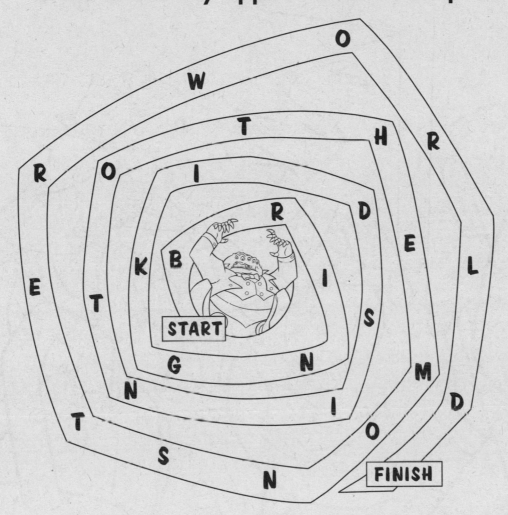

__ __ __ __ __ __ __ __ __

__ __ __ __ __ __ __ __

__ __ __ __ __ __ __ __ __

__ __ __ __ __ __ __ __

**Mike and the CDA heard what
Waternoose said. He's in big trouble now!**

Have a grown-up help you cut out each puzzle piece. Put the puzzle together to find out who is CDA Agent Number One. Tape the pieces together. Then color them.

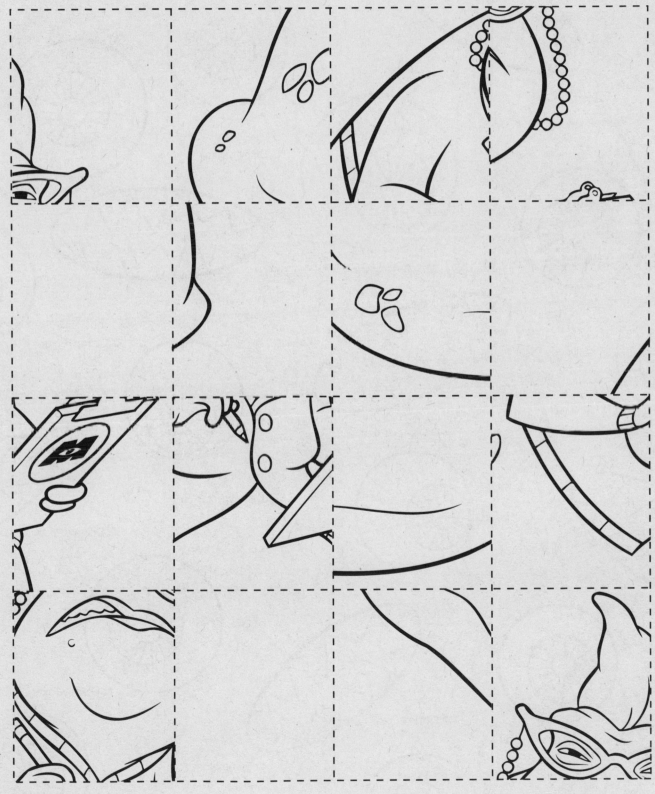

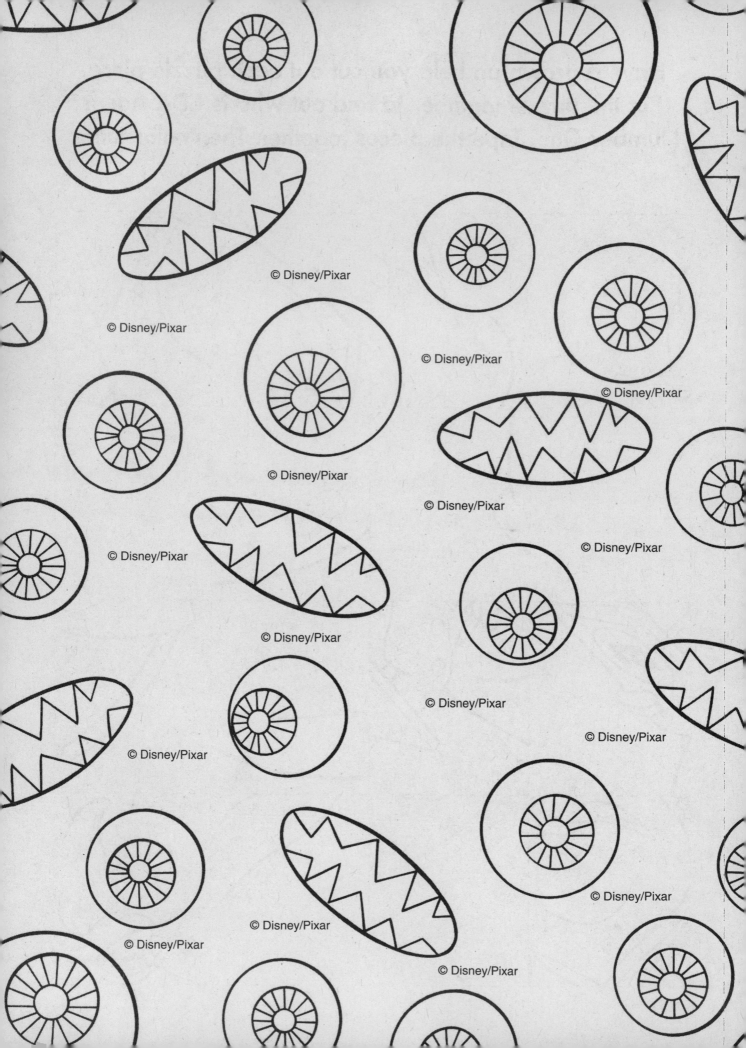

Waternoose is taken away—for good!

Now it's time for Boo to go home.
Sulley must say good-bye to her.

Thanks to Boo, Sulley has learned that children's laughs make even more energy than their screams. Now he's the boss at Monsters, Inc. He shows monsters how to make kids laugh.

Mike has a surprise for Sulley. It's Boo's door!

It's Nemo's first day of school. He can't wait!

Nemo has a weak fin.
Marlin thinks the ocean is not safe for his son.

TAD   PEARL   SHELDON

Mr. Ray, their teacher, is taking the kids on a field trip.
Marlin asks Mr. Ray to keep an eye on Nemo.

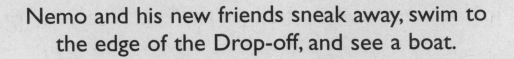

Nemo and his new friends sneak away, swim to
the edge of the Drop-off, and see a boat.

Marlin has followed Nemo to make sure he is safe.

To prove he is brave, Nemo wants to tag the fishing boat.
Help Nemo get there by finding a safe path through the maze.

Nemo touches the boat, but then a diver catches him!

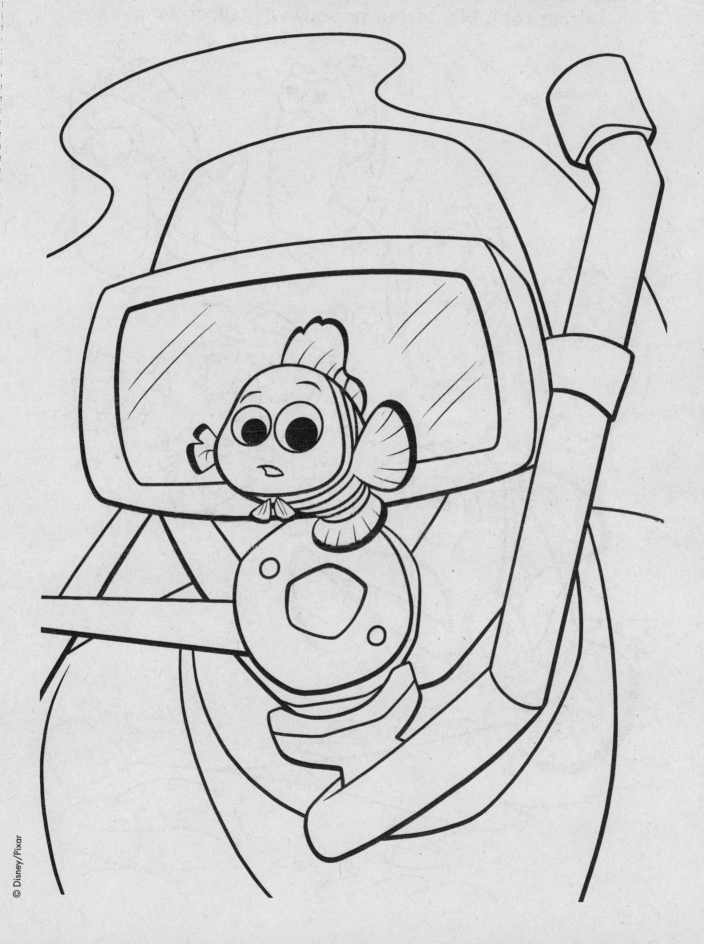

Marlin asks some fish if they have seen the boat that took Nemo, but nobody will talk to him.

A fish named Dory has seen a boat.
She tells Marlin to follow her!

Dory swims very fast. Marlin is afraid he will lose her. How many other fish can you count?

Dory has a bad memory!
She asks Marlin why he is following her.

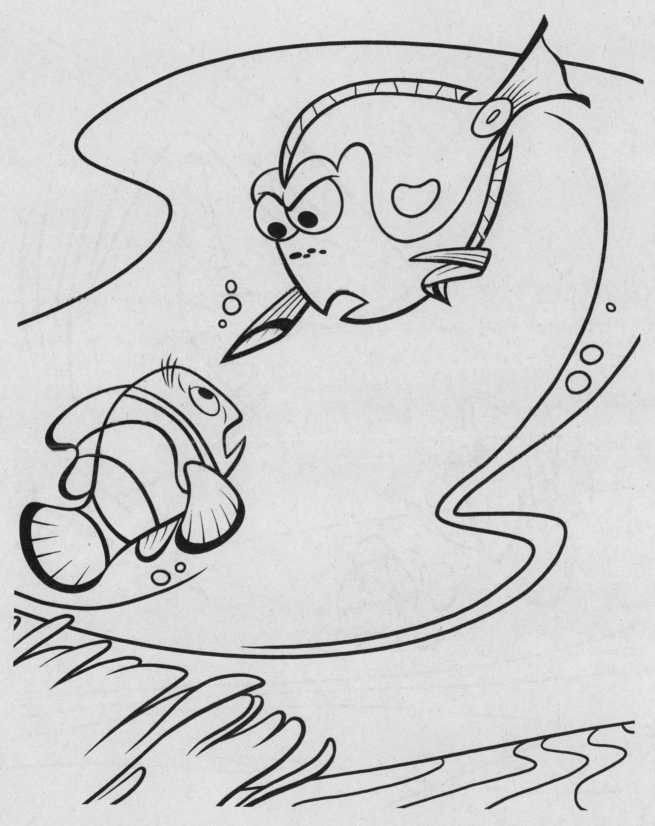

Marlin and Dory meet a shark named
Bruce, who invites them to a party.

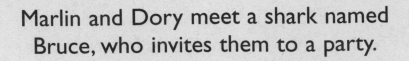

The party is for sharks who are trying to stop
eating fish. Marlin meets a new "chum" there.

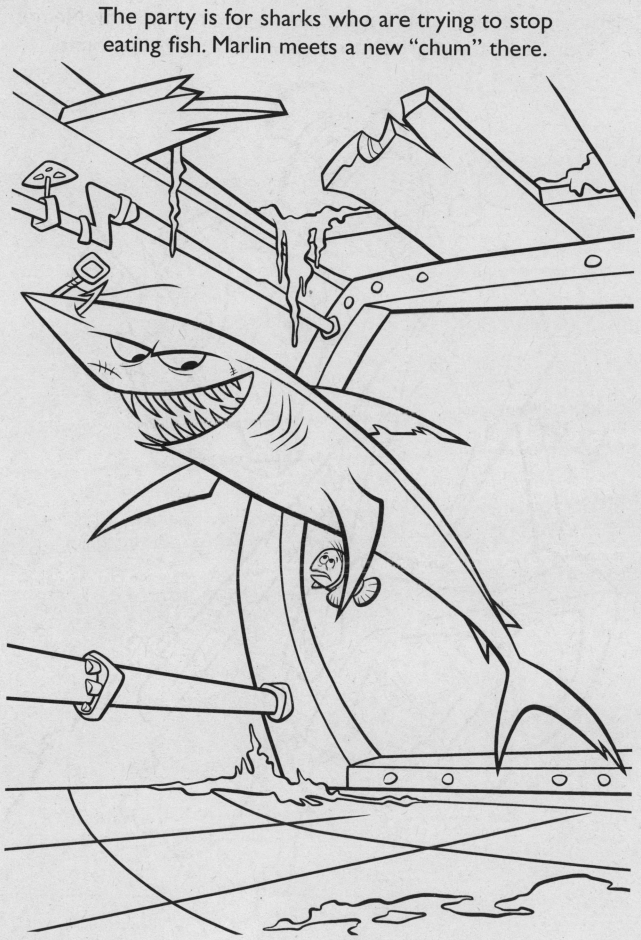

Marlin finds a mask that belongs to the diver who took Nemo!
Dory asks the sharks if they can read the writing on it.

But all Bruce wants to do is eat Marlin and Dory.
They escape while the other sharks try to stop Bruce.

Nemo has been taken out of the ocean.
He is now in a fish tank in a dentist's office.

Nemo tells the other fish he is from the ocean.

Nigel, a pelican, visits his fish-tank friends.

Nemo learns he will be a present for the dentist's niece Darla.
Gill, the leader of the tank, has an idea.

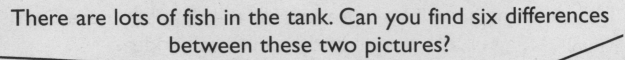

There are lots of fish in the tank. Can you find six differences between these two pictures?

ANSWER: In the second picture, the treasure chest is closed, the tiki head is missing some stripes, a plant has been added, Peach is upside down, Bloat is blown up, and the diver's helmet is closed.

Meanwhile, back in the ocean, Dory has dropped the mask!

Dory remembers that she can read. Use the code to read the writing on the mask.

A	E	B	D	H	M	N	2	P	R	S	4	W	Y	L
■	💧	☀	●	◆	◩	♣	▼	♥	★	◉	◗	☐	☾	▲

♥ . ◉ ◆ 💧 ★ ◩ ■ ♣

◗ ▼ ☐ ■ ▲ ▲ ■ ☀ ☾ ☐ ■ ☾ '

◉ ☾ ● ♣ 💧 ☾

ANSWER: P. SHERMAN, 42 WALLABY WAY, SYDNEY.

Gill makes Nemo an official member
of the tank and explains the plan to escape.

Back in the ocean, Marlin tells Dory that
he wants to look for Nemo by himself.

But Marlin really needs help. Dory asks
some nearby fish for directions to Sydney.

When they come to a trench, Dory wants to swim through it,
but Marlin tricks her into following him over it.

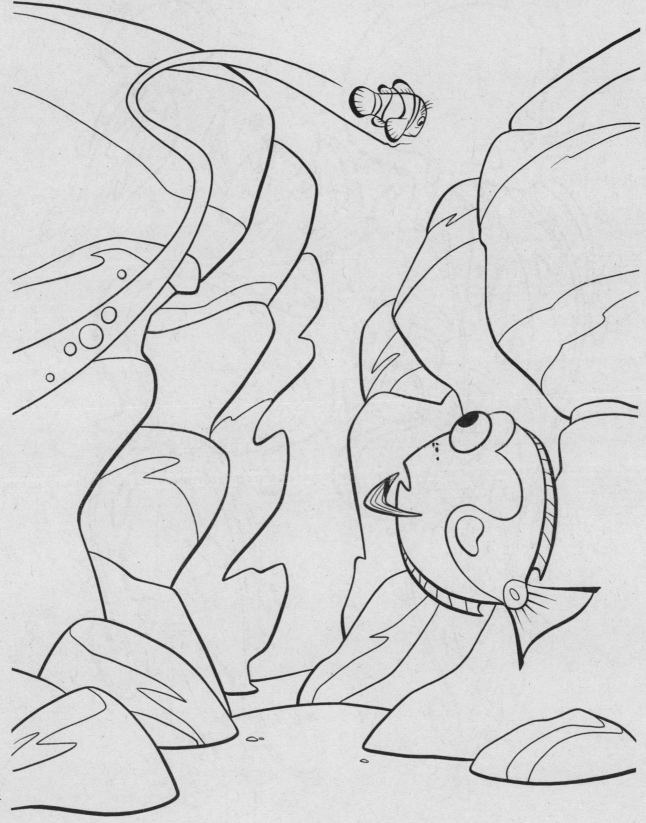

At the top of the trench, Marlin and Dory
are surrounded by jellyfish!

Marlin rescues Dory from the jellyfish.

Gill has a weak fin, just like Nemo!
He teaches Nemo how to be a strong swimmer.

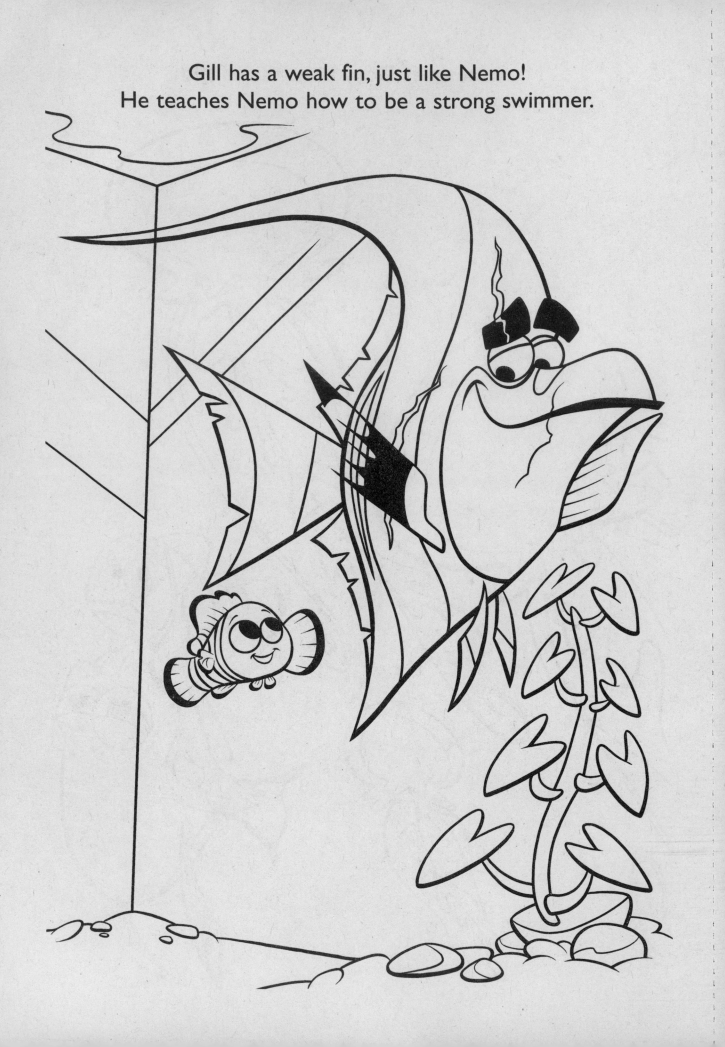

Part of the escape plan is to put a pebble in the filter
and let the tank get dirty. Then the dentist will need
to take the gang out of the tank to clean it.

The pebble falls out. The fish try to save Nemo.

Nemo is saved! Gill will not ask Nemo to try the plan again.

Marlin catches a ride. He tells his story, and the news spreads across the ocean!

**Dory plays hide-and-seek with the turtles.
How many baby turtles can you count?**

ANSWER: 8.

Finally, Nigel hears that Marlin is looking for Nemo.

Nemo learns that his dad is coming
to rescue him. He can't believe it!

Nemo is ready to try the plan again. Help him put the pebble in the filter so that he can escape.

Dory asks a whale for directions to Sydney.
The whale ends up swallowing Dory and Marlin!

Gill's plan is working—the tank gets dirty in no time!
Nemo is covered in algae!

Inside the whale's mouth, Dory and Marlin hang on to his tongue. They don't want to be swallowed!

The whale spouts Marlin and Dory into Sydney Harbor.

The next day, the tank gang wakes up
to a new filter—and a clean tank.

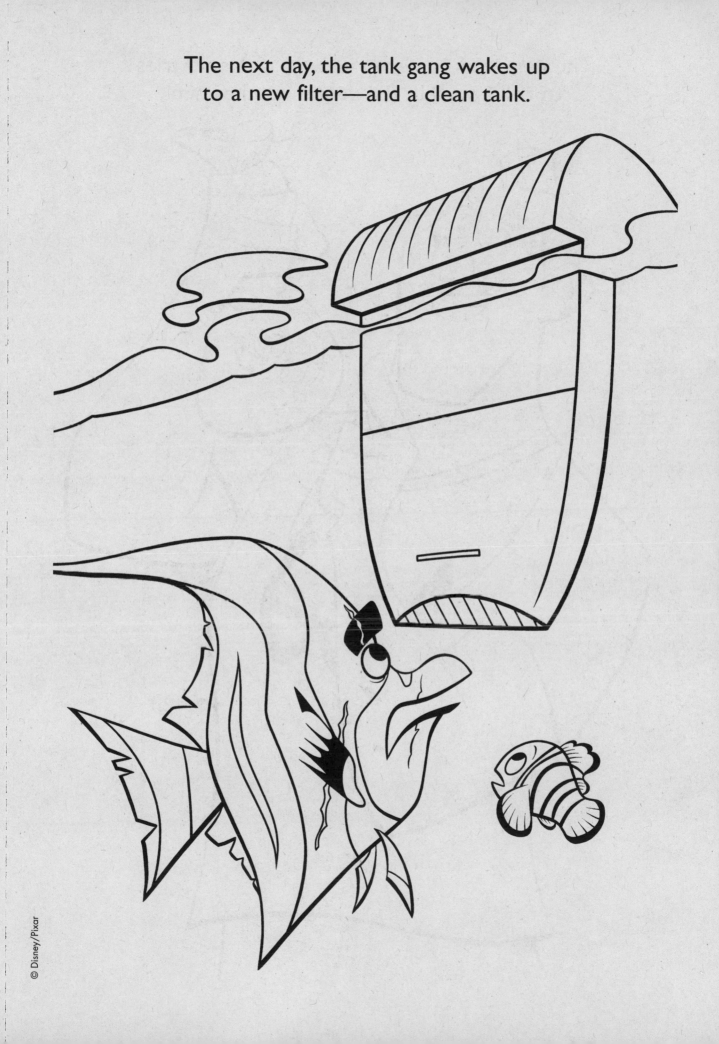

The dentist puts Nemo into a bag. Nemo tries
to roll away, but the dentist catches him.

Marlin and Dory have been searching all
night for Nemo, but it's a big harbor!

Oh, no! A pelican wants to eat Dory and Marlin.

Nigel comes to the rescue.

Nigel takes Marlin and Dory to Nemo.

It's Darla's birthday. She is ready for her present—Nemo!

Nemo plays dead, hoping the dentist will flush him down the toilet and free him. But the dentist takes him to the trash can instead!

Marlin thinks he has arrived too late. Look at this page
for sixty seconds. Then turn the page and see
if you can find four differences.

Nemo's bag breaks! Soon he won't be able to breathe.

Gill flips Nemo into the spit sink, and Nemo goes
down the drain and into the ocean. He's back
in the water and can breathe again!

Marlin tells Dory they were too late
and he must leave by himself.

Dory meets Nemo at last—
but she can't remember who he is!

Marlin finds Dory and Nemo! But then
Dory is caught in a net full of fish.

Nemo tells Marlin he has an idea. What does he want the fish to do? Use the code to find out!

D = ●   O = ◆   S = ◎

I = ★   M = ☐   W = ♥

N = ♣

___ ___ ___ ___   ___ ___ ___ ___ !
◎   ♥   ★   ☐   ●   ◆   ♥   ♣

It works! The net breaks, and all the fish escape.

Marlin and Nemo are finally back together!

Nemo and Marlin return home. And from
now on, Nemo will always listen to his father.

Freedom!

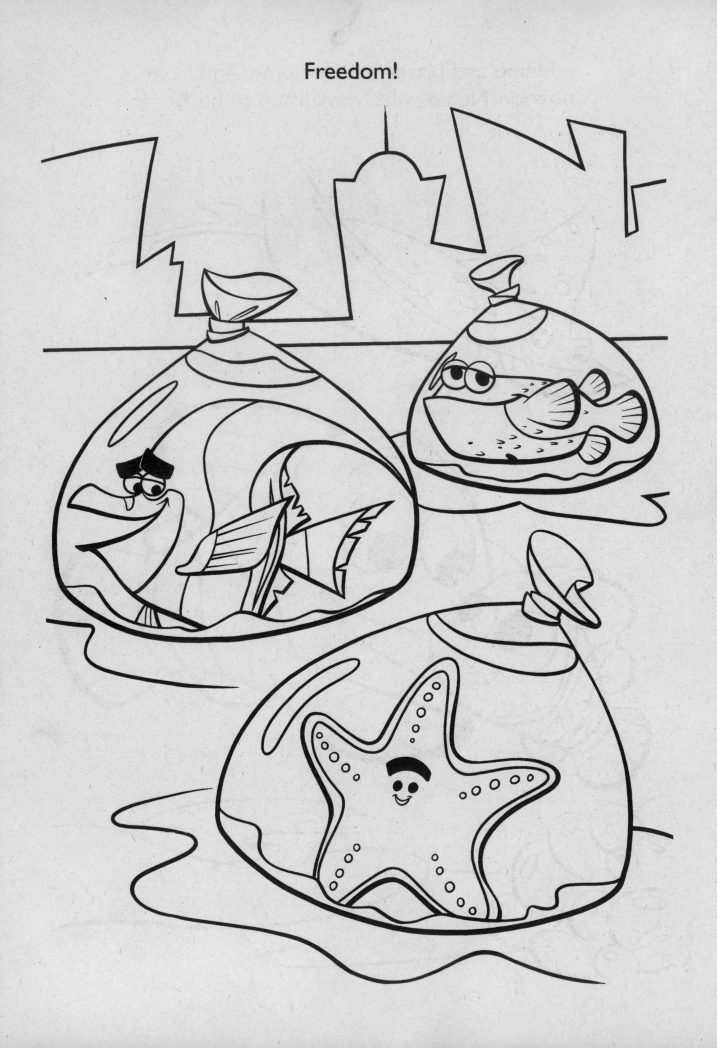

Mr. Incredible is the number-one Super!

He is always ready to battle evil in the world.

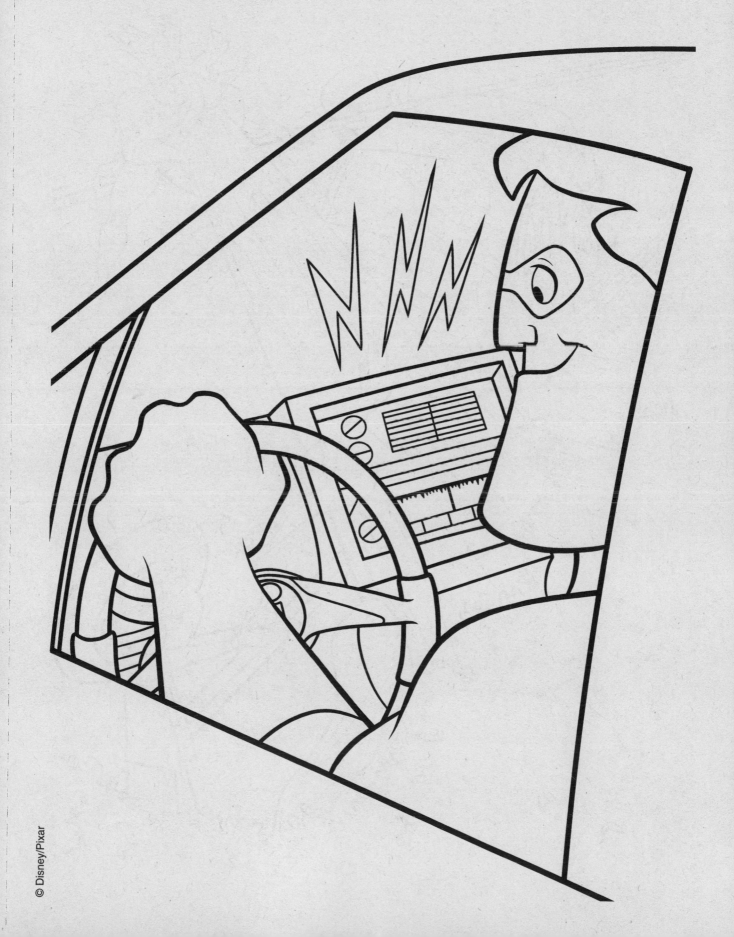

No job is too big or too small for Mr. Incredible.

Mr. Incredible's biggest fan, Buddy, wants to help his hero. To find out what Mr. Incredible tells him, close one eye and tilt the top of the page toward you.

ANSWER: I work alone!

Elastigirl beats Mr. Incredible to the punch! But there's something she thinks he needs to be. To find out what it is, circle every third letter. Then write the circled letters in order on the spaces below.

DCFGALRHEBQXTMIBUBNSLJPE

F l e x m b l e !

Frozone's Super skill helps him freeze bad guys.
He's Mr. Incredible's best friend.

Buddy tries to fly with his new jet boots,
but there's a bomb attached to his cape!
Mr. Incredible takes a wild ride to save him.

There's still more hero work to do before the day is done. Mr. Incredible saves a train full of people!

Will the city stay safe long enough for Mr. Incredible to kiss his bride? Hurry! Get him to his wedding on time.

START

FINISH

ANSWER:

Some people don't want to be saved. They think the Supers cause more harm than good! Hold this page up to a mirror to see what the newspaper headlines say.

ANSWER: Supers Sued!; Jumper Seeks Damages!

Mr. Incredible is forced to live in secret
as the not-so-incredible Bob Parr.

Sometimes Bob forgets to act like a normal guy.

Everyone in Bob's family has Super powers
except the baby, Jack-Jack. He's just good
at making a super mess at suppertime!

Bob's wife, Helen, used to be known as Elastigirl. Now she keeps the family under control with her Super-elastic arms. They come in handy when she's trying to stop fights between Super-fast Dash and Violet, who turns invisible and creates force fields.

Frozone has a new name, too. It's Lucius. Lucius is trying to leave his crime-fighting days behind, but Bob can't. Together, they listen to a police scanner.

Just like old times, Bob and Lucius
can *still* save the day.

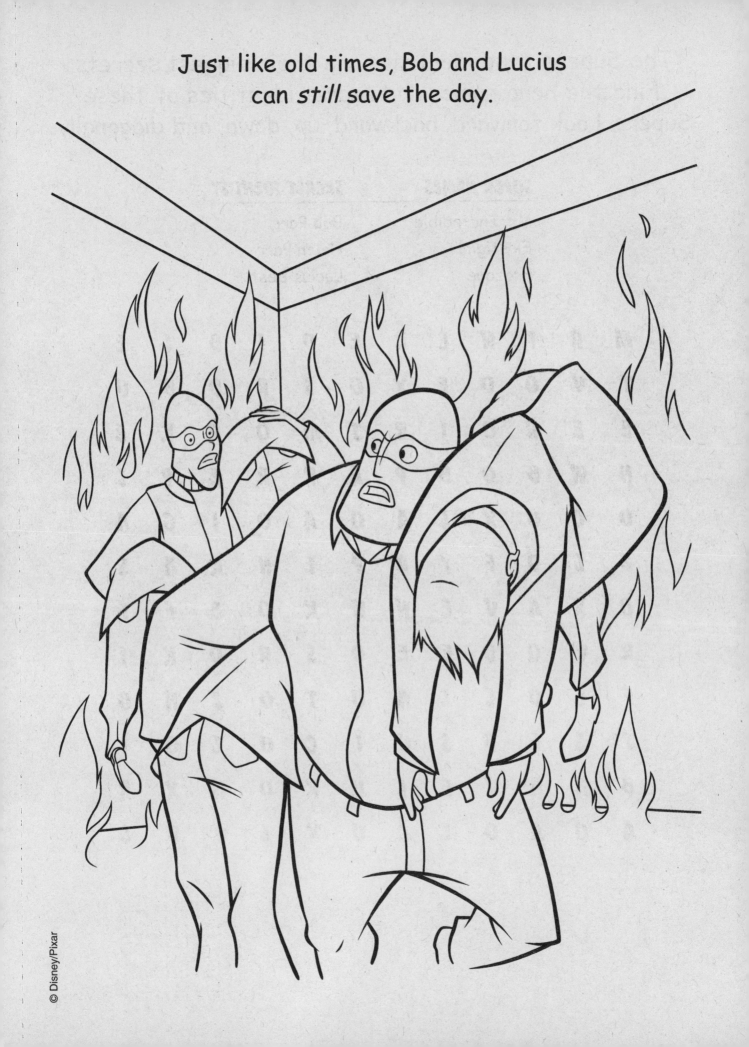

The Supers' true identities are their biggest secrets. Find the hero names and secret identities of these Supers. Look forward, backward, up, down, and diagonally.

SUPER NAMES	SECRET IDENTITY
Mr. Incredible	Bob Parr
Elastigirl	Helen Parr
Frozone	Lucius Best

```
M R I N C R E D I B L E
T V O D E X O S R D B U
E E R O I R T M O R K E
N W B O B P A R R E P L
O C U X L A U A O I G A
Z L D F Y R P E N K A S
O R A V E N H K O E F T
R V O D E E O S R D K I
F C U L L A U T O Z H G
T S E B S U I C U L O I
B H A V E L H K O N X R
A U A O I C U X L V D L
```

A mysterious woman named Mirage works for an old fan of Mr. Incredible. She has a secret message for Bob.

Bob's boss, Mr. Huph,
is not happy with Bob's work.

Bob gets frustrated with Mr. Huph.

Luckily, Mirage offers Bob a job.
He'll work as Mr. Incredible to stop
the Omnidroid, a learning robot.

Mirage takes Bob to the island of Nomanisan.

Mirage's jet drops Mr. Incredible on the island,
where he is attacked by the Omnidroid.

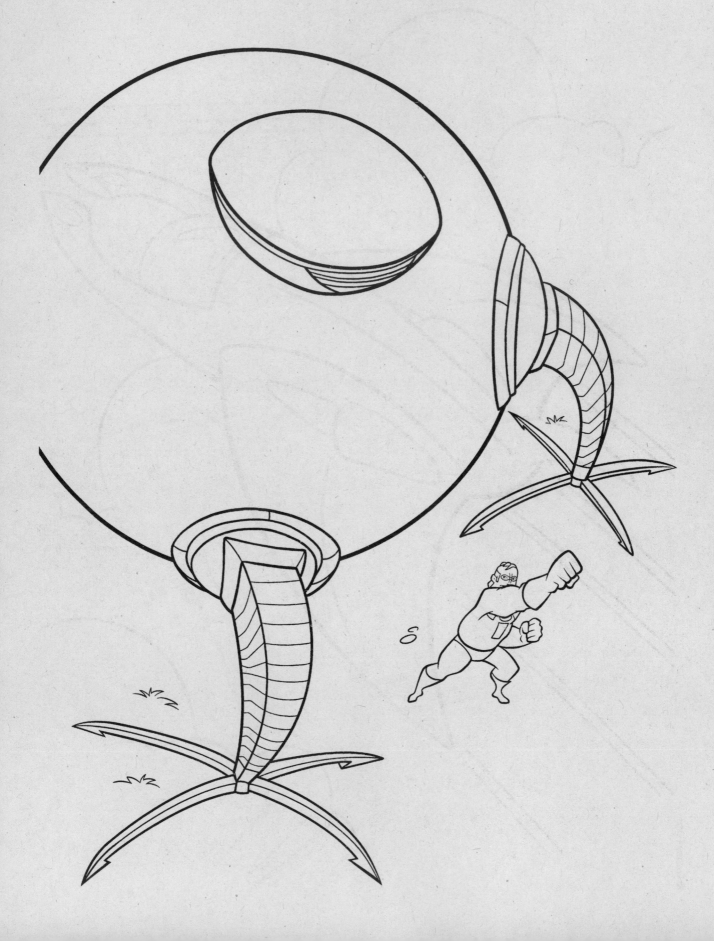

Mr. Incredible fights back and wins!
Mirage and a mysterious man watch him
on a computer screen.

Back home, Bob works out lifting trains.
He wants to be as strong as he used to be.

Bob needs some extra-special help with his Super suit.
To find out the only person who can do the job, close
one eye and tilt the top of the page toward you.

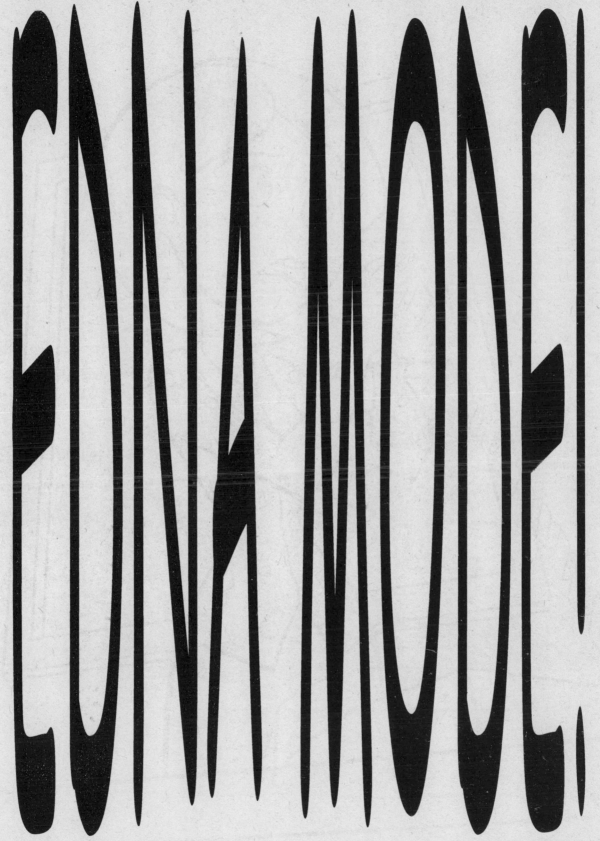

ANSWER: Edna Mode!

With a new suit ready, Bob takes on another
assignment. Helen hears Bob on the phone
and wonders what he is up to.

Use the code below to find out the name of
the evil genius who wants to destroy the Supers.

A	B	C	D	E	F	G	H	I	J	K	L	M	N	O	P	Q	R	S	T	U	V	W	X	Y	Z
1	2	3	4	5	6	7	8	9	10	11	12	13	14	15	16	17	18	19	20	21	22	23	24	25	26

___ ___ ___ ___ ___ ___ ___ ___ !

19   25   14   4   18   15   13   5

ANSWER: Syndrome!

Mr. Incredible discovers he has been working
for a villain! The evil Syndrome sends a bigger,
smarter Omnidroid to capture Mr. Incredible.

Syndrome takes Mr. Incredible prisoner.

Mr. Incredible makes a daring escape.

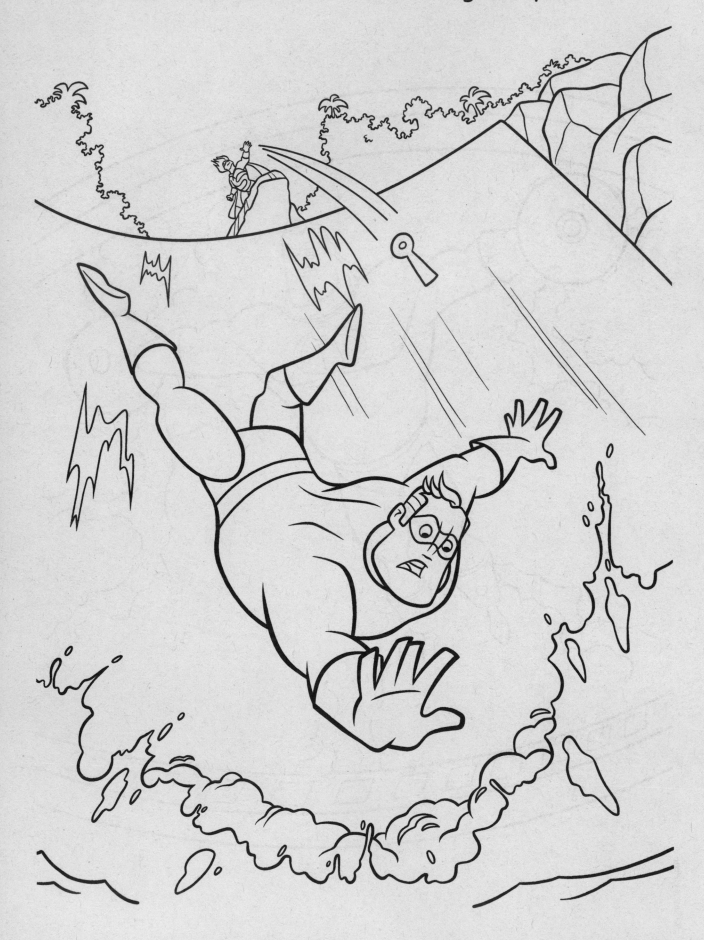

Underwater, Mr. Incredible finds a message
from a missing Super, Gazerbeam. Find out
what it says by replacing each letter with the
one that comes before it in the alphabet.

L S P O P T !

_ _ _ _ _ _ _ !

ANSWER: Kronos!

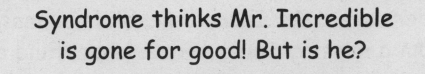

Syndrome thinks Mr. Incredible
is gone for good! But is he?

Not a chance! Mr. Incredible gets
busy doing what he does best.

Back at home, Helen pays a visit to Edna Mode. Edna tells Helen she has designed Super suits for the entire family. She also shows Helen a device that tracks where all her Super family members are.

Mr. Incredible discovers Syndrome's computer.
Could the password be *Kronos?*

Helen wants to know where Bob is.
She activates the tracking device.

Mr. Incredible's luck has run out!
Syndrome captures him once again.

Helen rushes to find Mr. Incredible. Meanwhile, the kids discover their new Super suits.

Look out, world! Dash is ready for action.

Helen heads off in her jet
to the island of Nomanisan.

Mr. Incredible watches helplessly
as Syndrome attacks Helen's jet.

Elastigirl finds some
unexpected guests on board.

Syndrome's weapons just miss Helen and the kids.

Elastigirl turns into a parachute
to get her kids to safety!

Elastigirl tells Dash and Vi to use their
Super powers if they get into any trouble.
Then she heads out to save Mr. Incredible.

Elastigirl is stretched to her limits
at Syndrome's headquarters.

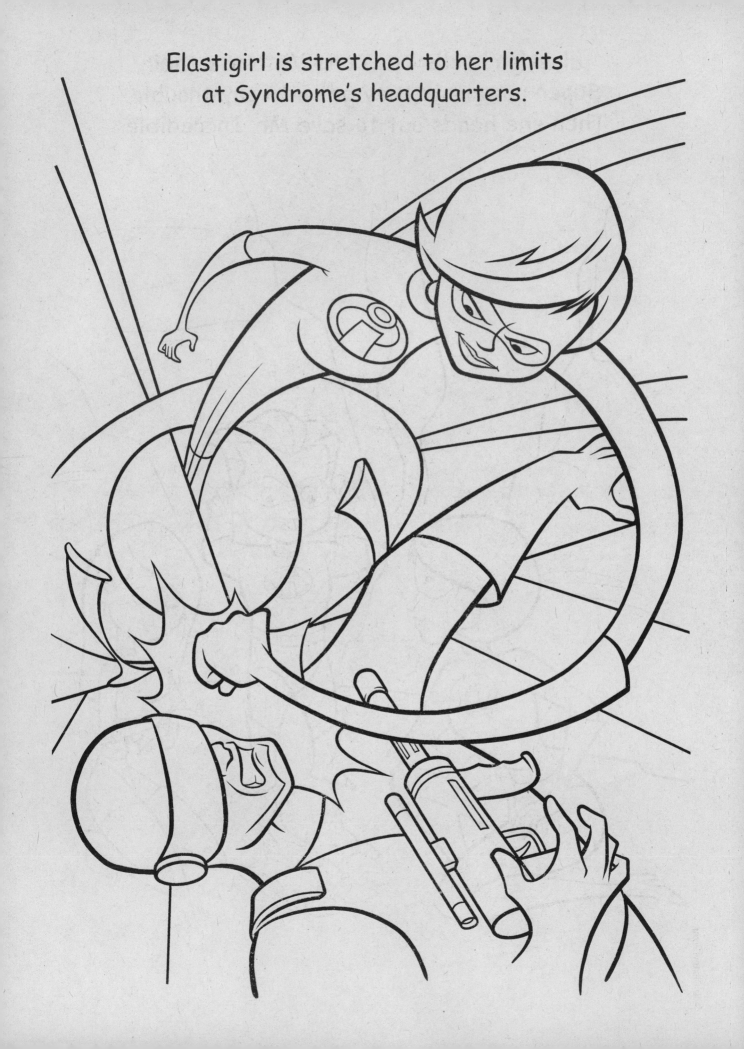

Mr. Incredible is happy to see his wife. But their get-together is cut short when Mirage tells them that Dash and Vi set off one of Syndrome's alarms.

Mom and Dad to the rescue!

Mr. and Mrs. Incredible show Dash and Vi how it's done!

Unfortunately, Syndrome is always one
step ahead of the Incredible family.

Syndrome reveals his evil plan. When he sends
the Omnidroid to the big city of Metroville,
he will be the only one who knows how to defeat it.
Then he will look like the world's best Super.

Mirage helps the Incredibles escape in a rocket. Help guide them to a safe landing so they can save the city from the Omnidroid.

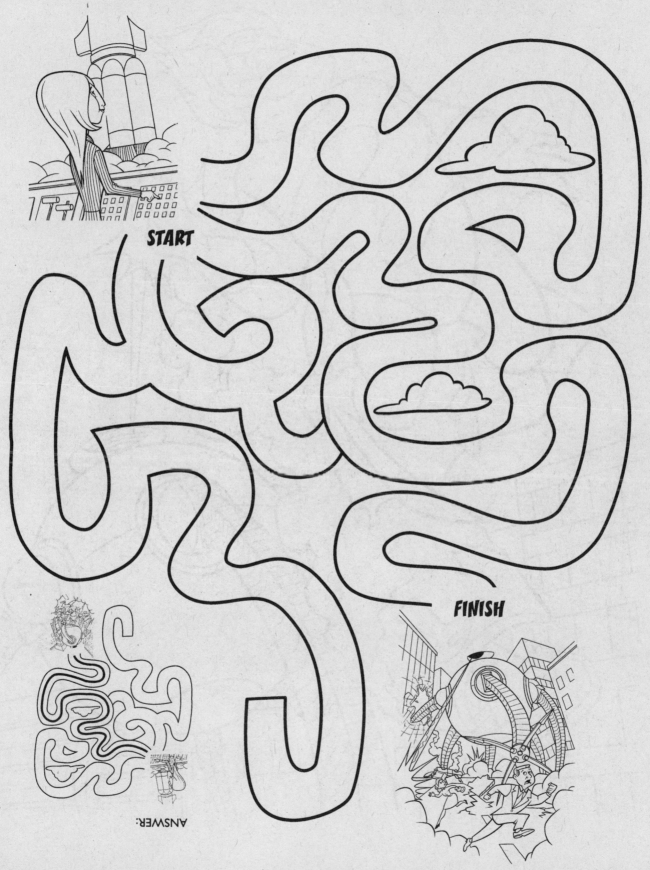

START

FINISH

ANSWER:

Syndrome learns that trying to be
a Super is harder than it looks.

Mr. Incredible's family does not want him
to try to defeat the Omnidroid alone.
They will all work together.

Mr. Incredible throws the Omnidroid's
remote device to Dash.

Teamwork wins as the Supers
save the day once again!

The Supers are back!

Upset at his defeat, Syndrome takes Jack-Jack.
But the baby shows that he is truly an Incredible!

Elastigirl turns into a parachute
to save her littlest Super, Jack-Jack.

It's back to normal for the Parr family.

Once again, it's time to be Super!

Ramone is an artist in Radiator Springs. His custom paint jobs are the best.

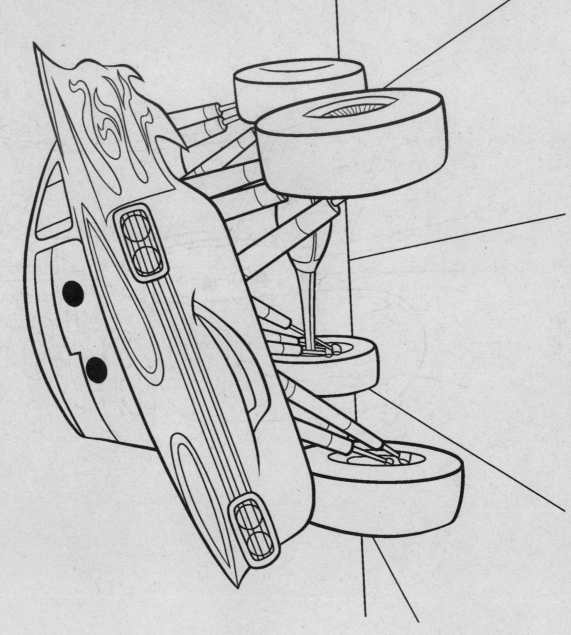

Fillmore makes his own organic fuel.

Sarge owns the local supply shop.

Luigi has tires to fit every car, and he's always ready to make a deal.

Guido may be small, but no one can change a tire faster than he can.

Mater is a tow truck. His name is like "tuh-mater", but without the "tuh."

Mater is friendly to everybody, but McQueen is his best friend.

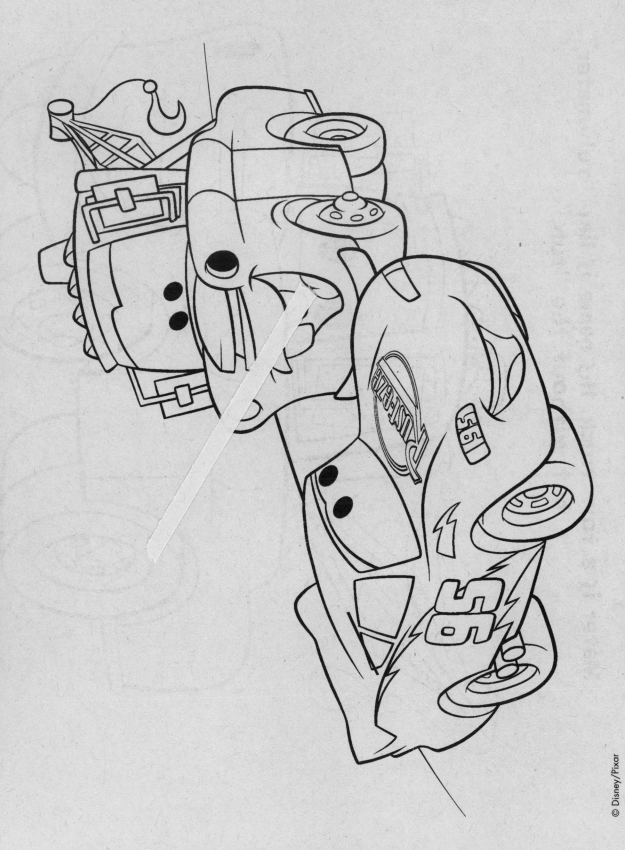

The King is the world's greatest racing champion.

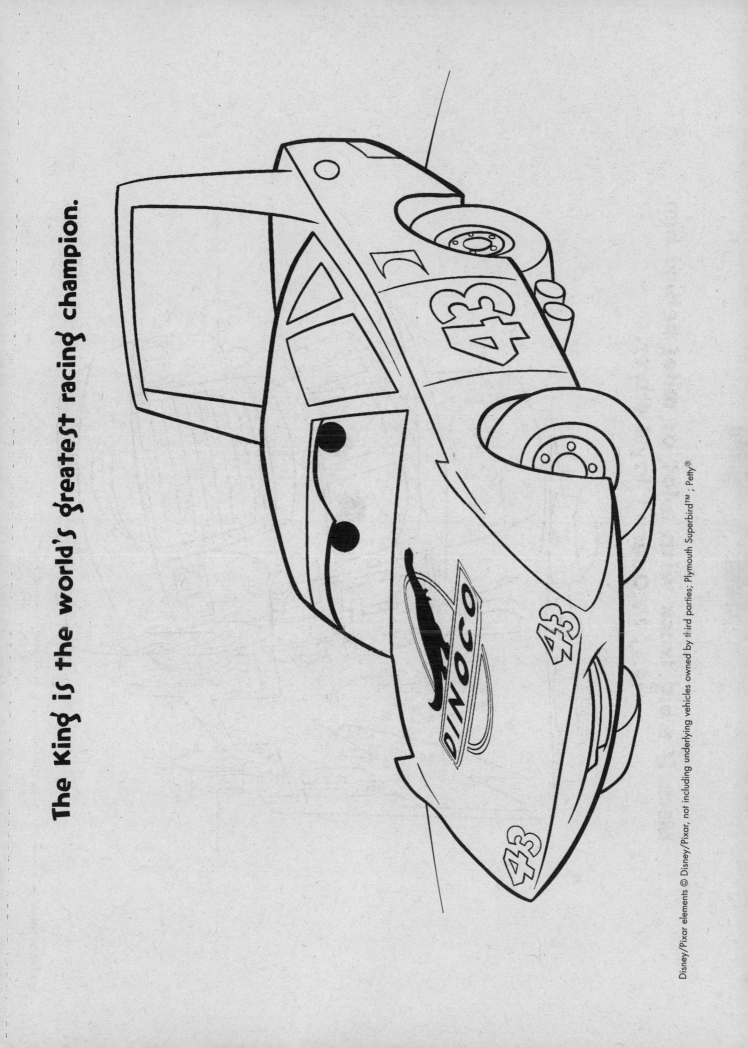

Mack is a big truck with a lot of miles behind him. He is McQueen's loyal driver.

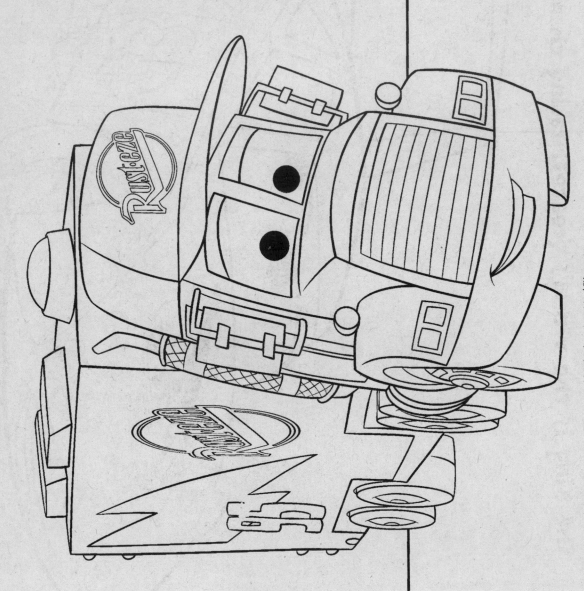

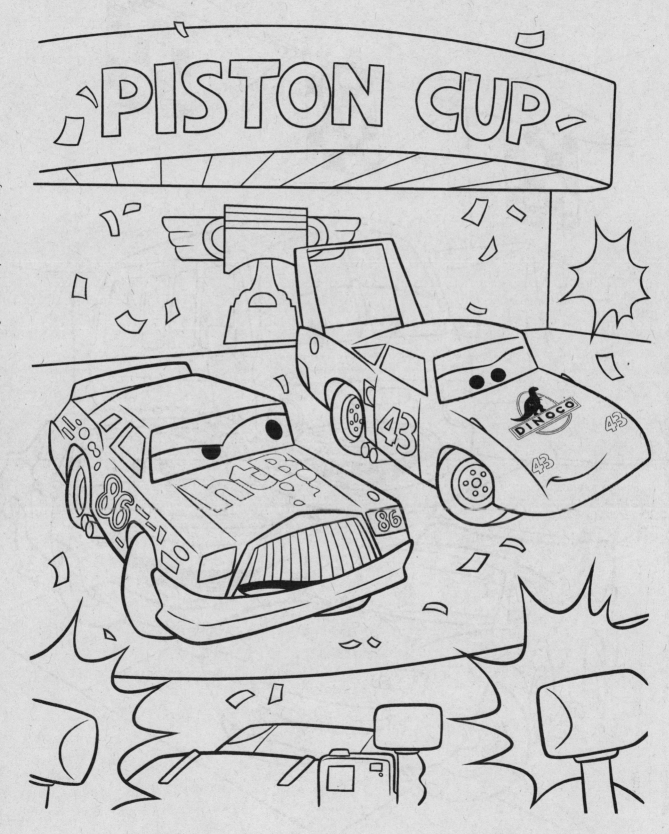